FACE ART

Lynsy Pinsent

From cowboys to clowns, ladybugs to leopards,
15 amazingly original designs for the perfect children's party.

ISBN 0-439-32287-1

This book was designed and produced by Quarto Children's Books Ltd. The Fitzpatrick Building, 188-194 York Way, London N7 9QP. Copyright © 2001 Quarto Children's Books Ltd.

All rights reserved. Published by Tangerine Press™, an imprint of Scholastic Inc. 555 Broadway, New York, NY 10012. All rights reserved.

Scholastic and Tangerine Press™ and associated logos are trademarks of Scholastic Inc.

No part of this work may be reproduced, stored in a retrieval system, or transmitted in any form or by any means, electronic, mechanical, photocopying, recording, or otherwise, without written permission of Tangerine Press™. Requests for such permission should be addressed to Tangerine Press, 1080 Greenwood Blvd., Lake Mary, FL 32746

Printed in China

12 11 10 9 8 7 6 4 3 2 1
0 1 2 3 4 5 6/0

Contents

INTRODUCTION
Preparation 4
Basic Techniques 6
Using a Make-up Chart 10

ANIMALS
Leopard 11  
Tiger 14 
Dog 16 
Cat 18 
Ladybug 20 

CLOWNS
Baby Clown 22 
Card Clown 24

HALLOWEEN
Pumpkin 26 
Skull 28 
Dracula 30 
Wicked Witch 32

CARNIVAL
Batman 35 
Cowboy 36 
Pirate 38 
Spiderman 40

— PREPARATION —

Preparation

Face art is loads of fun! Just follow the easy steps in this book, and soon you'll be creating some amazing designs. But before you begin, you need to get familiar with a few basics. Get to know the tools of the trade and practice a few techniques and you'll soon become a great face artist!

Your kit contains everything you need to start face painting:

- Water based face paints
- Applicator stick
- Make-up Sponge
- Easy-to-follow steps
- Black face crayon
- Brush

Sponges
Use the make-up sponge to apply large areas of color. It is best used slightly damp. Use the applicator stick for small areas of color and for large details. A professional "stipple" sponge is good for applying beard stubble, but a plastic scouring pad will give the same effect.

Brushes
Use the brush for applying smaller areas of color. As you go on, you may like to add different brushes to your kit – for example, some artists like to use a fine brush for line work and for adding detail.

Look after your brush by washing it gently in soapy water after each session.

Colors
The paints and crayon are water-based. The colors can be mixed easily and they dry very quickly on the skin. When you have finished, your design can be easily removed with soap and water.

— PREPARATION —

Preparation tips
★ Use a copy of the Make-up chart on page 10 to plan your design on paper first.
★ Collect everything you need and set it out in front of you.
★ Protect your work surface with a towel or cloth.
★ Make sure your model sits at a convenient height for you.
★ Have a mirror close by, so you can check that your make-up design is even and balanced.
★ Wrap a towel around your model's shoulders to protect the clothes.
★ Keep the model's hair off the face with hair clips or a hairband.

! **Caution**: Do a patch skin test before you begin. Dab a bit of paint on the inside of the wrist. If there is no reaction after an hour or two, you should be safe to proceed.

Special effects
★ Some spooky faces require a full white base (see Skull, page 28, and Dracula, page 30). Try to apply it as thinly as possible. This will prevent it from becoming muddy when any other colors are added.
★ When painting animal faces (see pages 11-21), keep a picture of the real animal nearby to inspire you to imitate the real thing as accurately as possible!

Have handy:
- Cotton swabs
- Hair clips/hairband
- Soap
- Water jar
- Facial tissues
- Make-up chart and pencil
- Waste basket or bag
- Towel
- Mirror

Application tips
★ Always begin with a clean, dry face.
★ Wash your sponge between colors, or use a piece of sponge for each color (ordinary bath sponge is fine).
★ Make sure you don't put the paint on too thickly.
★ Apply the lightest colors first, then progress to the darker ones.
★ Wait until a color is dry before applying the next one.
★ Blend colors with a clean, damp brush or by stippling with a barely damp sponge.
★ Take extra care near the eyes. If necessary, ask your model to keep their eyes closed.
★ Do not rush. It takes time to make a great face. Symmetrical shapes and neat lines are the essence of good make-up.

As you develop your skill, you can add to your palette with fluorescent paints, glitter paints and more colors!

— BASIC TECHNIQUES —

Basic Techniques

Applying a base

Tip: Use a damp sponge to apply a full-face base. It is much quicker and gives a smoother finish than a brush. To avoid streaks or patchiness, make sure the sponge is not too wet.

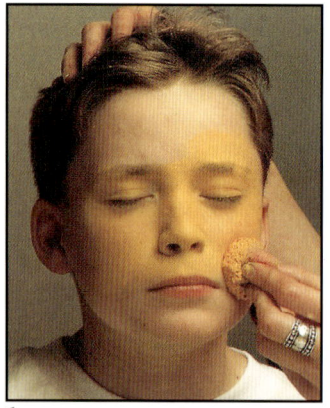

1 If you want a duotone base, always apply the lightest color first – yellow in this case.

2 The yellow base reaches almost to the hairline.

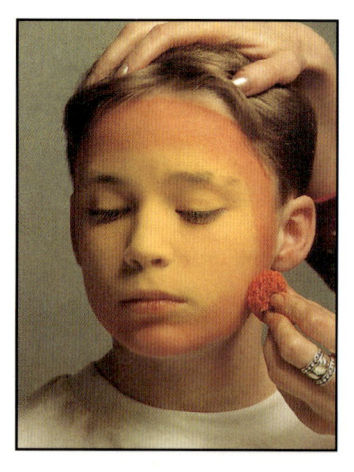

3 Blend an orange border into the yellow by lightly dabbing ("stippling") along the adjoining edge with a barely damp sponge.

Tip: Dark skins can sometimes be harder to cover than lighter ones. Stipple the base color over the entire face with a barely damp sponge.

4 The finished duotone base.

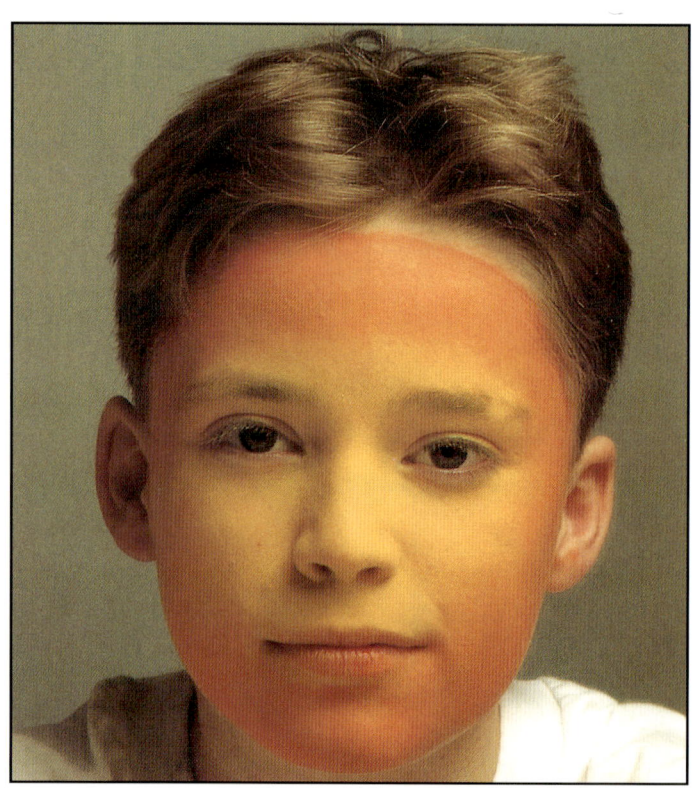

— BASIC TECHNIQUES —

Painting the eyes

Tip: Always take great care when painting anywhere near the eye. Ask the model to close their eyes if necessary. If you need to get closer to the bottom eye-line, the model should look up and away from the brush as you do so.

Tip: Fine lines can also be drawn using a face crayon instead of a thin brush. To fill in an area of color, you can outline it with a crayon and fill it with a brush or sponge.

Tools of the trade:
Defining the eyes with black paint can look very dramatic. Then add white highlights for striking effect.

Method 1

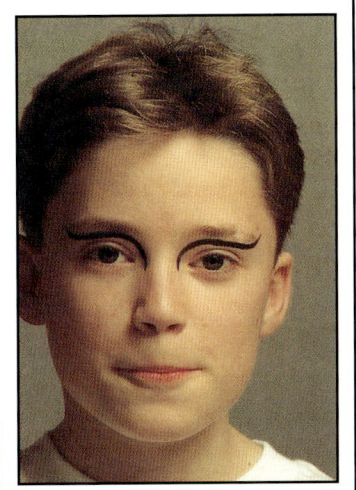

1 This method is ideal for very young children because it starts beside the nose and sweeps across the brow without actually touching the eye.

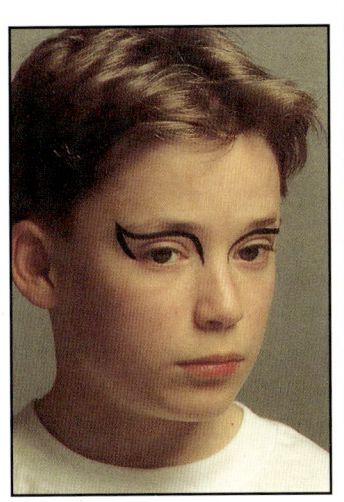

2 You can enhance the effect by simply bringing the end of the line down to meet the outer corner of the eye.

Method 2

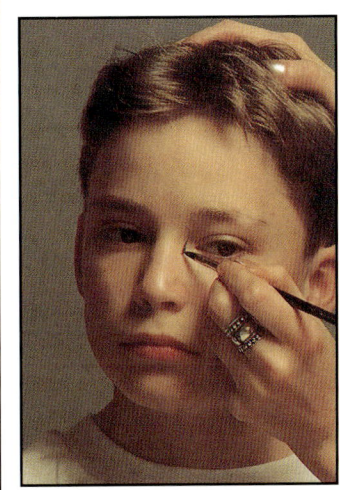

1 For a more elaborate image, use a fine, thin brush and start the top line just below the inner corner of the eye.

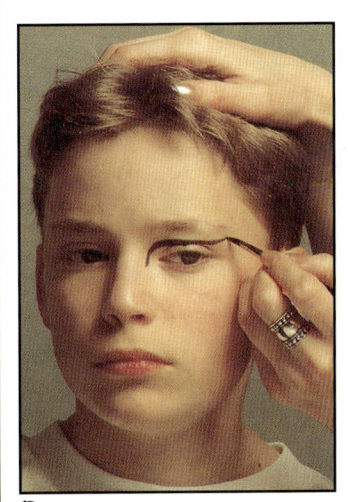

2 Take the line across the eyelid, winging it up slightly at the end.

— BASIC TECHNIQUES —

3 Bring the end of the top line down to the outer corner of the eye.

5 Start the bottom line at the inner corner and sweep it beneath the lower lashes to join the outer corner of the top lid.

Method 3

1 Shape the top lid using the method described previously.

4 Fill in the outlined area in black.

6 The finished effect.

2 Start the lower line below the inner corner and sweep it up, following the direction of the top lid, to finish parallel to, but not touching, the top line. The space between the two lines can be emphasized with a slick of white paint.

★ This "open-ended" technique is often used in the theater because it makes eyes appear larger.

— BASIC TECHNIQUES —

Five O'Clock Shadow

1 To create an unshaven look, use a small coarse sponge to stipple black/brown paint gently over the beard and mustache area of the face.

2 The finished effect.

Tip: Build up the depth of color very gradually. Tap the sponge on the back of your hand before each application of color to remove any excess paint. If any areas look too dark, stipple them lightly using a paler color.

Eyebrows

A change of eyebrow shape can transform a face into a multitude of different characters. Think about the type of personality you are trying to convey. Make faces in the mirror – of laughter, anger, sadness – and see what happens to your features. Build up a repertoire of shapes based on what you observe.

1. Sad

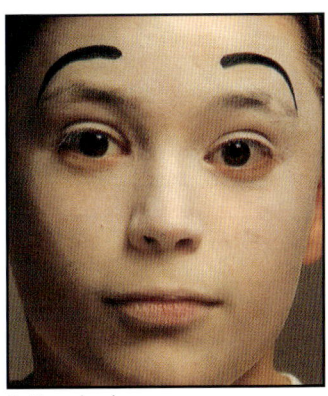

2. Surprised

3. Cruel

9

— BASIC TECHNIQUES —

Using a Make-up Chart - A Finished Example

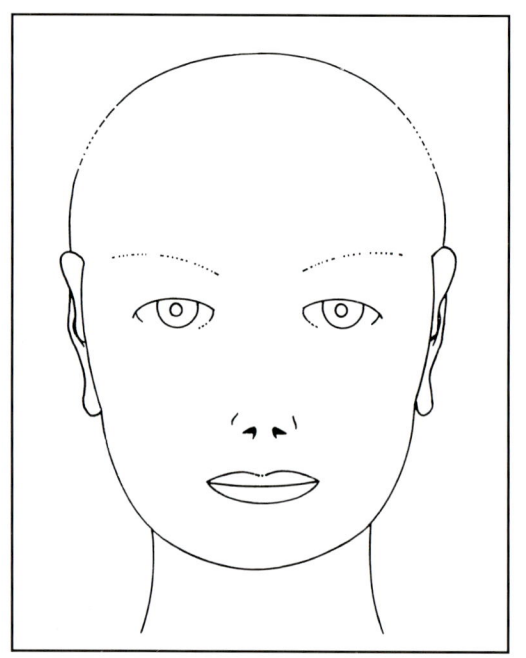

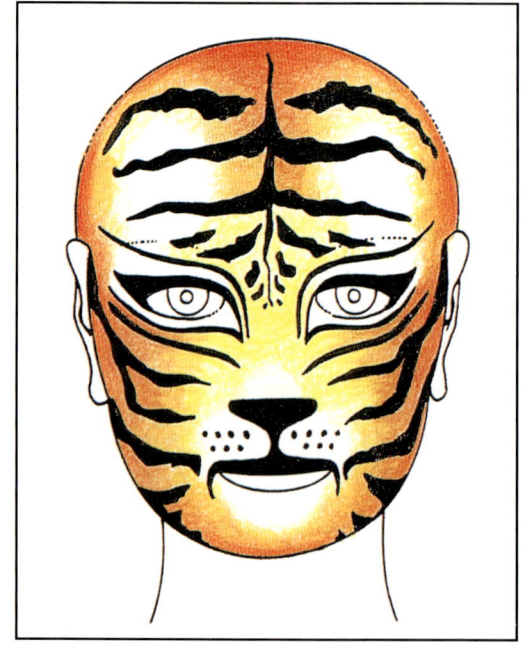

1 You can photocopy this blank chart to help you plan your own creations.

2 Fill in the design with paint, felt tip pens, or colored pencils.

3 Keep referring to your chart as you apply the makeup.

— ANIMALS —

Leopard

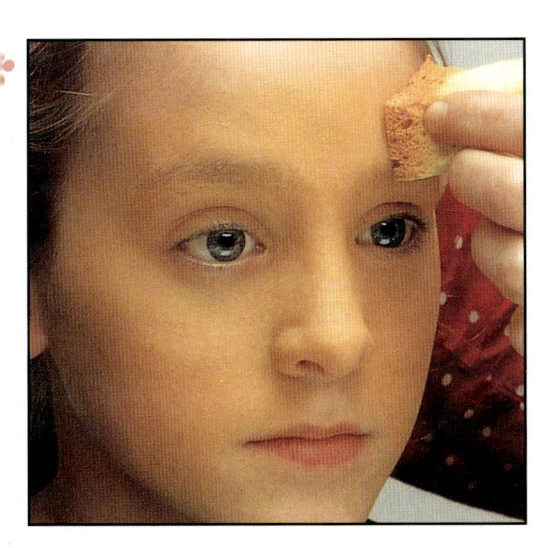

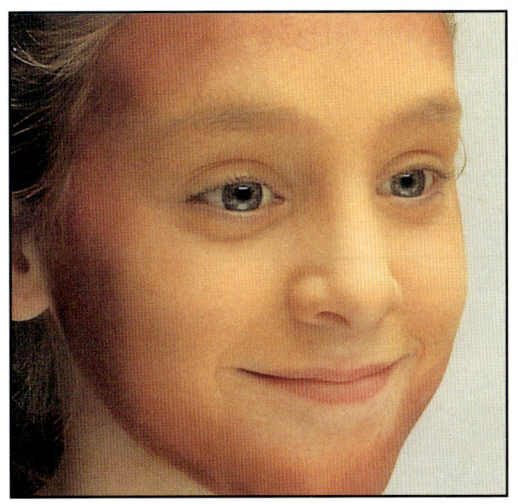

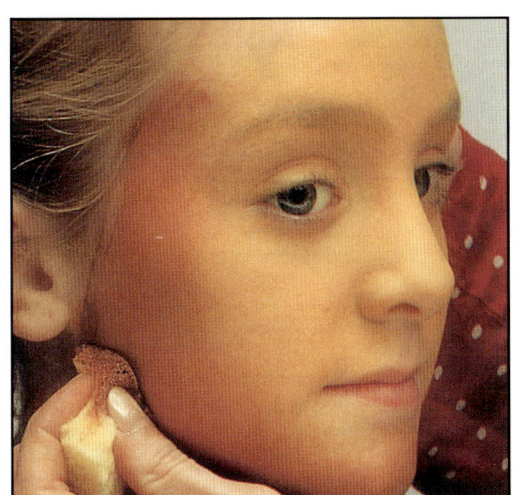

1 Dab yellow base color over the whole face using a sponge.

2 Use another sponge to shade the outer parts of the face with medium-brown, made by mixing yellow, orange, red and blue.

3 Merge the yellow and brown colors together by stippling gently with the yellow sponge.

Tip: When stippling colors to blend them, keep the sponge almost dry; squeeze it onto a facial tissue to remove any excess moisture.

4 Stipple white paint with a sponge over the mouth and chin area, and from each eyebrow up to the hairline.

— ANIMALS —

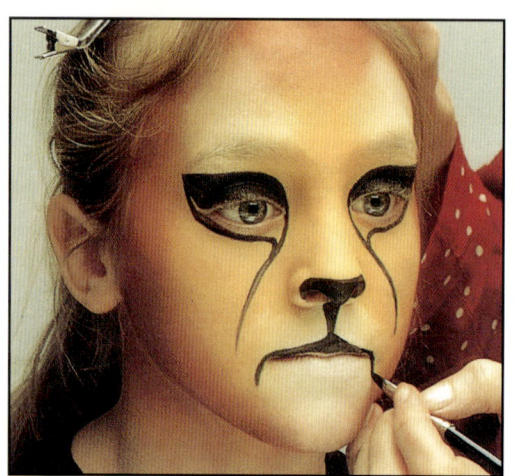

5 With a thin brush, paint black across the whole eyelid. Start at the inner corner of the eye, take the line past the outer corner, and wing it up slightly at the end.
★ Paint a black line from the inner corner of the eye, taking it down over the cheek.
★ Paint a black line below the bottom eyelashes, starting at the inner nose line. Follow the direction of the top lid, sweeping the end of the lower line up to meet it at the outer corner.

6 Paint the tip of the nose black. Draw a thin line from the center of the nose down to the top lip. Paint the top lip only in black, dropping the ends down at each corner of the mouth. Block out the bottom lip completely with white.

7 Already the model has a real animal look; this is because the main features of the face – the eyes, nose, and mouth – have been de-humanized to a large extent. Once this effect has been achieved, the image is set, and any further decoration is incidental. This is why you must follow the preliminary stages so carefully.

8 Having added the whisker spots to the top lip with black, paint on some leopard markings in brown mixed with black, highlighting them just off-center with flecks of white.

12

— ANIMALS —

9 Remember, most animal markings are symmetrical.

10 The finished leopard.

— ANIMALS —

Tiger

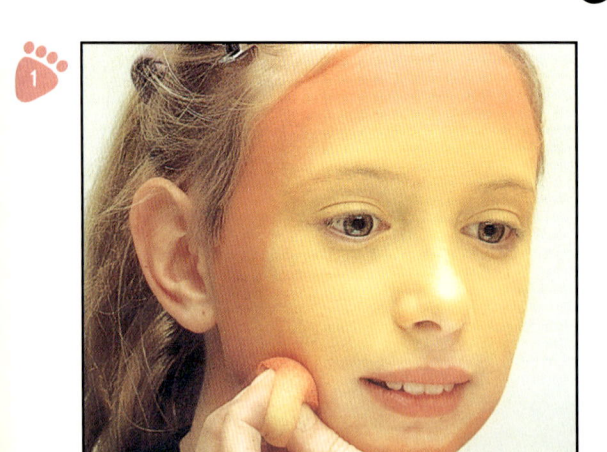

1 Apply a base of yellow with orange on the outer edges. Stipple the colors together with a sponge.

2 Stipple on white patches around the mouth and above the eyebrows. Paint the eyes in black, starting just below the inner corner; take the color across the lid and wing the line up slightly just past the outer corner of the eye. Paint the lower eyeline below the lashes, following the curve of the top line, but leave the outer end open.

★ The mouth and nose are applied in the same way as for the leopard (see page 11) except that the tiger's nose should be extended a little way onto the cheek.

3 For the tiger's stripes, use a narrow brush to paint black lines across the forehead. Finish one side of the face first, then copy the design onto the other side to keep the pattern symmetrical.

14

— ANIMALS —

4 The finished tiger. Because the markings are so strong, there is no need to add whiskers – these would only clutter the face and spoil the effect.

— ANIMALS —

Dog

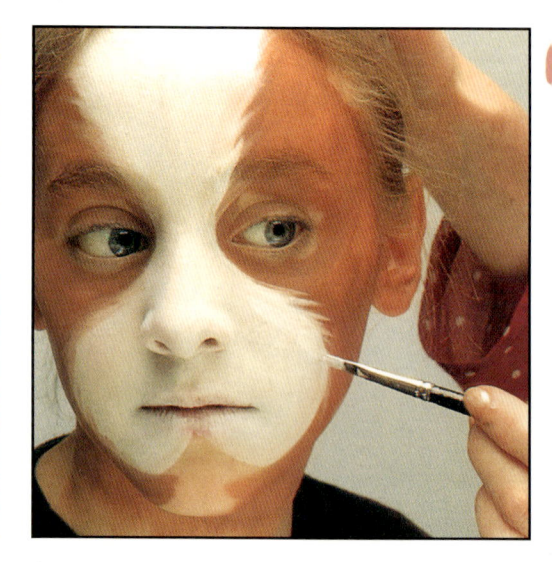

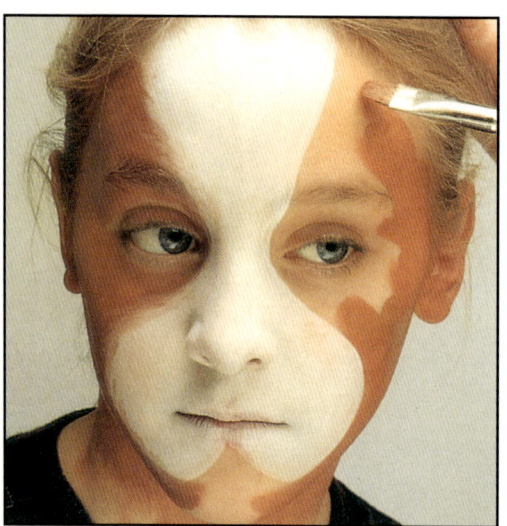

1 Using a flat, wide brush, paint a white shape down the center of the face as shown.

2 Fill in around the white with a medium-brown color.

3 Soften the line where the two colors meet by gently feathering the white onto the brown with a very fine brush.

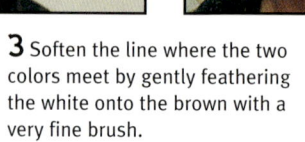

4 Mix some orange and blue to make a dark brown color. Carefully paint the eyes in a dark brown, using jagged, uneven brush strokes.

— ANIMALS —

5 Use black for the mouth, extending the line beyond the corners of the mouth before dropping it sharply to the chin. Paint the tip of the nose black and add some black whisker spots.

6 The drooping tongue is dark red. Fleck the eye areas with red and yellow to highlight them. Finish off by painting the chin in dark brown from the centre outward and upward using jagged brush strokes.

— ANIMALS —

Cat

1 Cover the face with white paint blended into a red border by stippling with a damp sponge.

2 Paint the upper eyeline in black, starting just below the inner corner of the eye, following the lash line and sweeping the end of the line out and up. The lower line is also black, and follows the curve of the upper one, sweeping up to join it at the outer edge. Fill in the whole eyelid area in black.

— ANIMALS —

3 Use small, delicate brushstrokes to create the eyebrows, making sure their shape follows that of the eyelines. Paint in some similar lines along the outer edge of the lower eyeline.

4 Paint the tip of the nose black, taking the center line down to the top lip. Paint along the top lip and curl the ends of the line up slightly onto the cheek. Add some black whisker spots.

5 Around the edge of the face, apply some rough strokes of black. Highlight this shaggy effect, and the area below the eyebrow, with patchy dashes of yellow. Draw a small dark red semicircle on the bottom lip.

6 A very glamorous cat.

— ANIMALS —

Ladybug

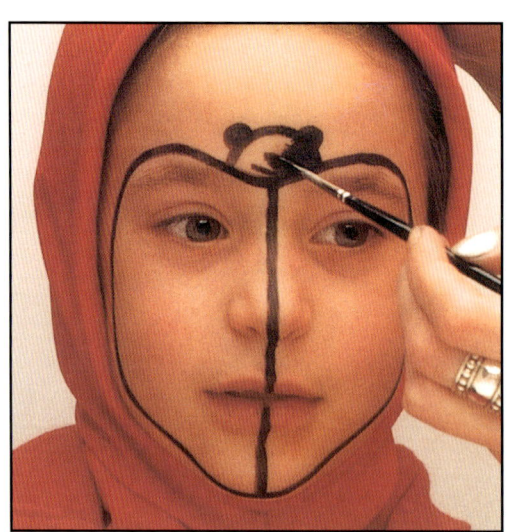

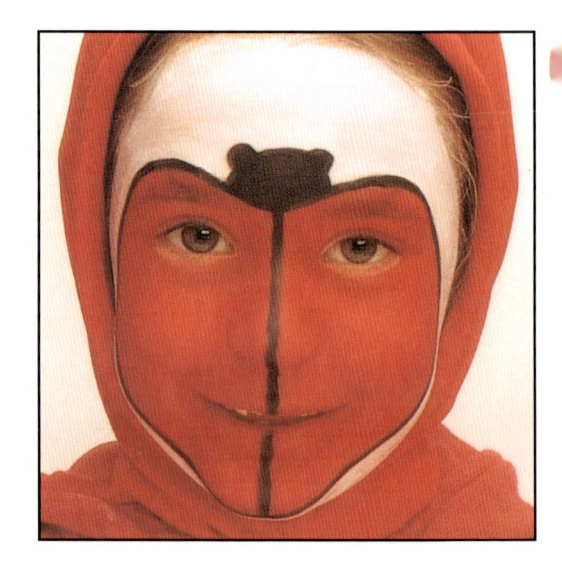

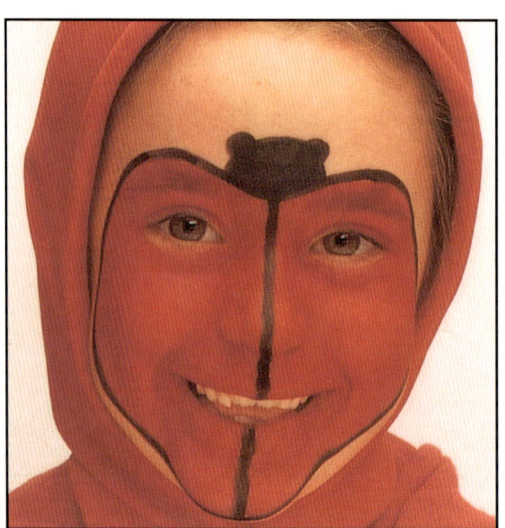

1 Using a thin brush, carefully paint the black outline onto the face.

2 Fill in the shape with red, using a flat, wide brush.

3 Paint the borders of the face in white, taking great care not to let the colors overlap.

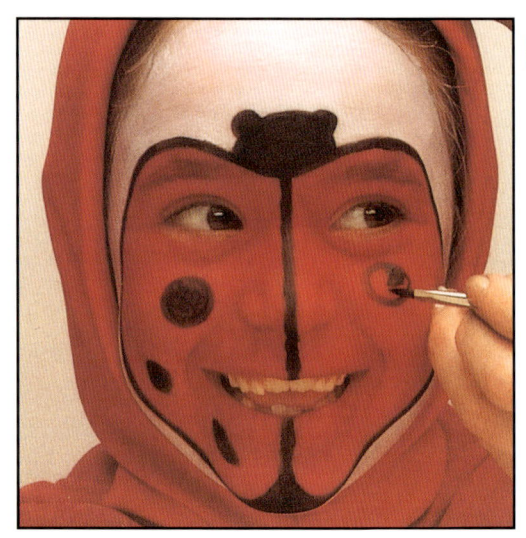

4 Add the black spots and a small black triangle on the chin.

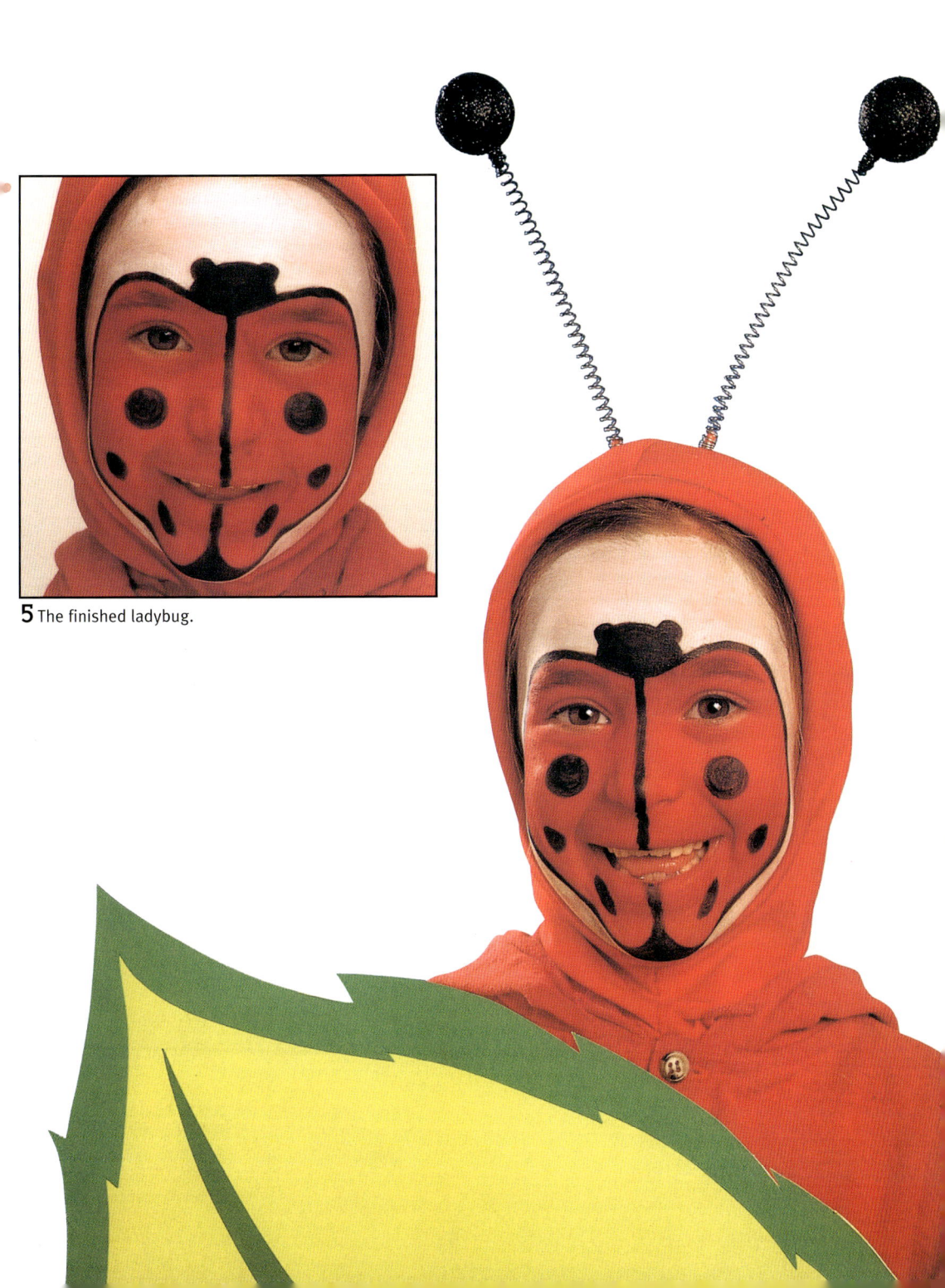

— ANIMALS —

5 The finished ladybug.

— CLOWNS —

Baby Clown

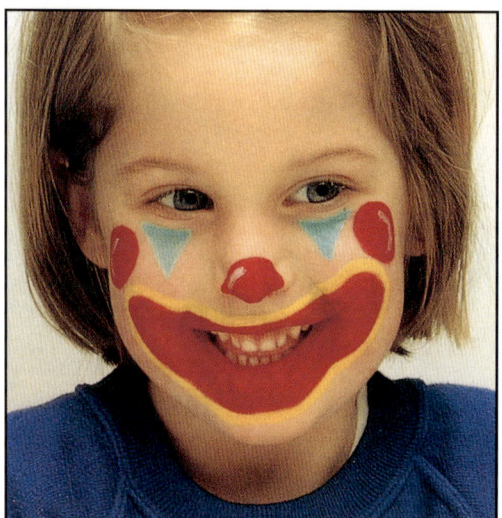

1 Paint on a wide red smile, and add a red dot on each cheek and a red tip to the nose.

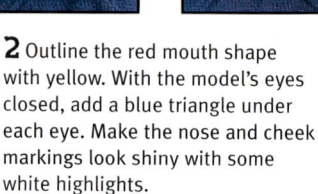

2 Outline the red mouth shape with yellow. With the model's eyes closed, add a blue triangle under each eye. Make the nose and cheek markings look shiny with some white highlights.

3 Mix the red and blue to make purple, and paint on some arched purple eyebrows. Add a dash of white above each eye.

4 A very cheerful clown face.

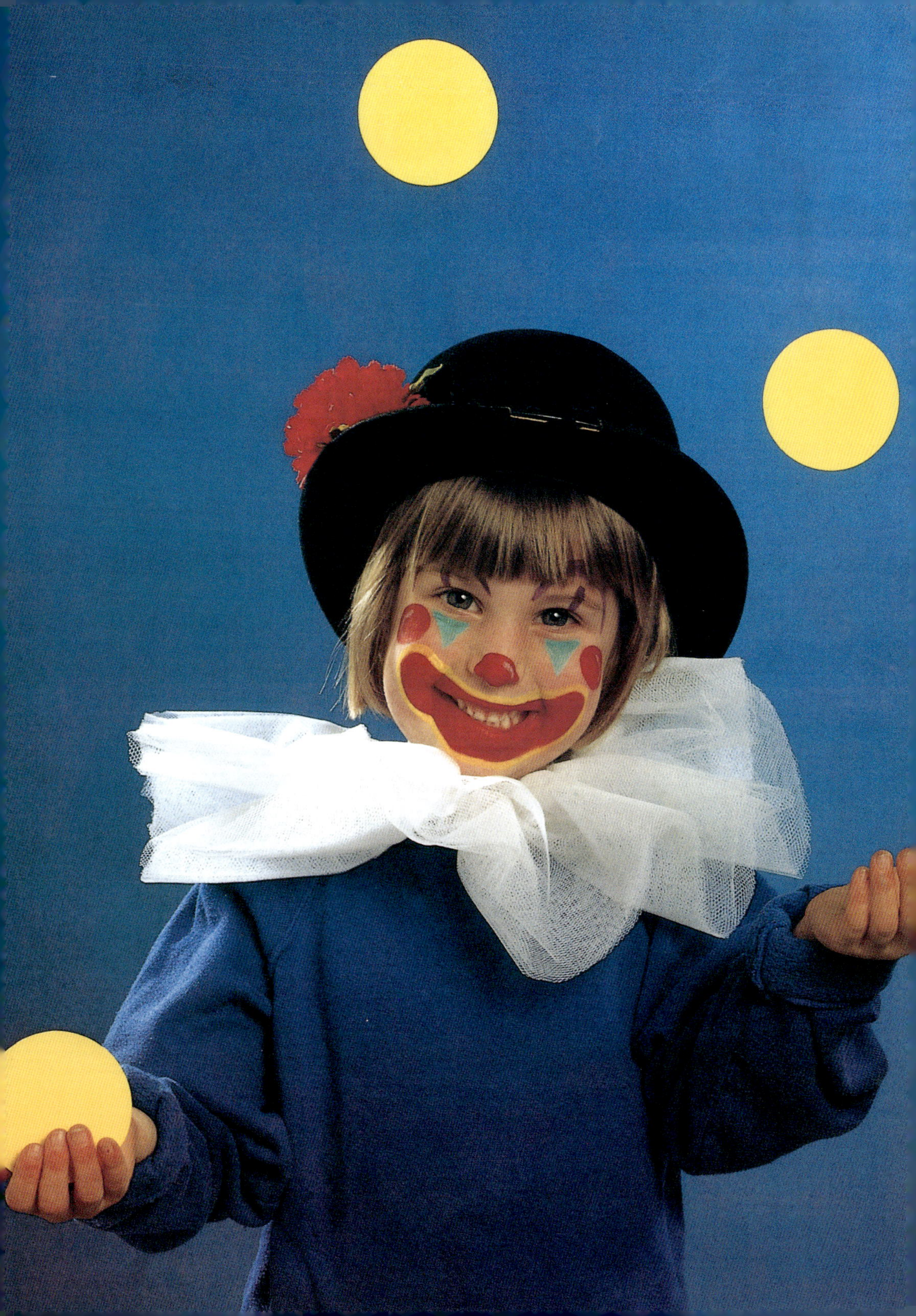

— CLOWNS —

Card Clown

1 Sketch the design lightly onto the face with a black eye pencil. Once you are satisfied that both sides of the face are even, trace over the design with the brush.

2 Use the brush to make a white outline around all the inner shapes of the design.

3 Fill in the remaining areas with white.

4 Paint the diamond shapes black, including the eye shapes but leaving the eyelids blank.

— CLOWNS —

5 Color the shape on the lips in red.

6 Carefully paint the borders of the face and the stripe down the nose in red.

7 Outline the eyes in white. Whenever you are working close to the lower lid, ask the model to look up and away from your hand.

— HALLOWEEN —

Pumpkin

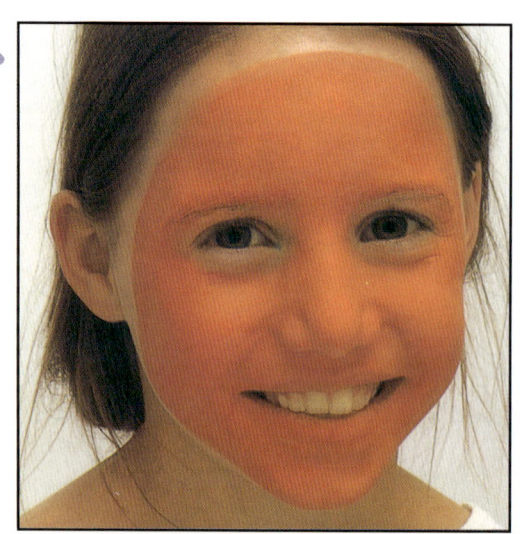

1 Paint a large orange circle over the whole face, filling in the color with a sponge.

2 Add a black triangle over each eye, using a fine brush. Extend the points of the triangle below the line of the lower lid and carefully fill in the center, leaving a margin around the eye.

3 Paint another triangle on the tip of the nose and extend the sides out onto the cheeks.

4 Outline a huge smile in black and make the top edge a zigzag line.

— HALLOWEEN —

5 Fill in the whole mouth shape with black.

6 Design a small brown pumpkin stalk in the middle of the forehead and run some segment lines down from it, following the curve of the orange outline.

— HALLOWEEN —

Skull

1 Cover the whole face in white using a sponge. Draw in the outlines for the nose and eye sockets in black.

2 Fill in these areas in black, leaving a small segment of white showing at the center of the nose.

3 Feel for the model's temple hollows (just away from the eye area on either side of the head) and emphasize them by painting a black semicircle over each one.

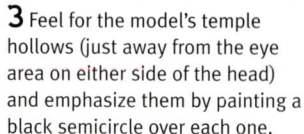

4 Feel for the cheekbones and paint along the underside, stopping approximately level with the center of the eye. Then drop the line down to the jawline. Fill in the area behind this line with black.

— HALLOWEEN —

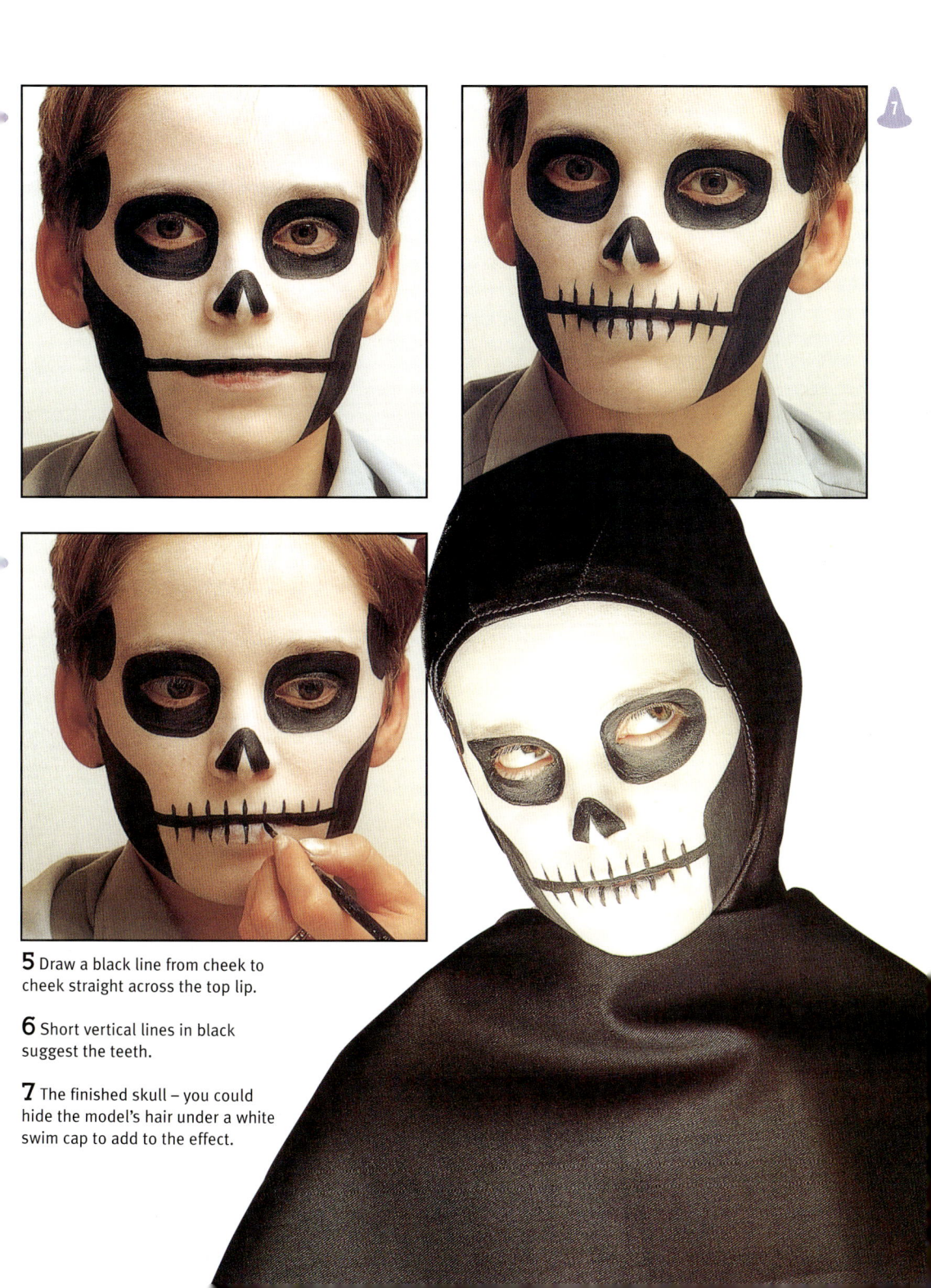

5 Draw a black line from cheek to cheek straight across the top lip.

6 Short vertical lines in black suggest the teeth.

7 The finished skull – you could hide the model's hair under a white swim cap to add to the effect.

— HALLOWEEN —

Dracula

1 Cover the face with white, gently stippling over any patchy areas with a sponge. Add some angular black eyebrows, brushing up with light feathery brushstrokes.

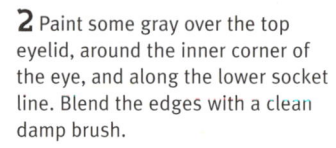

2 Paint some gray over the top eyelid, around the inner corner of the eye, and along the lower socket line. Blend the edges with a clean damp brush.

3 Draw the outline of long pointed vampire fangs over the bottom lip, using a fine brush or a sharpened black face crayon.

4 Fill in the fangs in white and the surrounding lips in black.

30

— HALLOWEEN —

5 Use a brush or a cotton swab to smudge some red paint along the lower eyelash line. The model should look up and away from you while you do this. Shade the cheek hollows with light gray, using a sponge or a brush. Powder eye shadow could be used instead of paint, but powder colors are usually less dense than paint and do not last as long.

6 Add trickles of blood from the fangs and the corners of the mouth.

— HALLOWEEN —

Wicked Witch

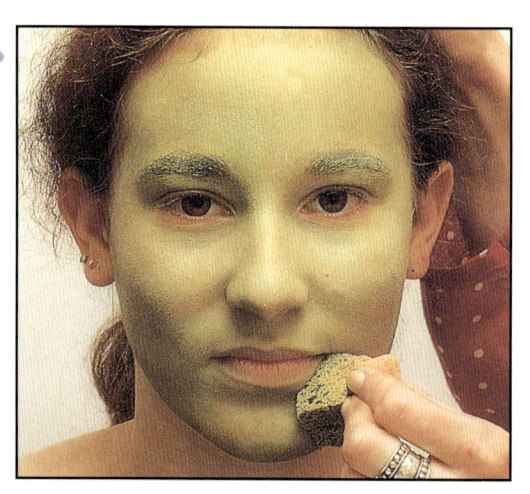

1 Use a sponge to cover the whole face in yellow. You can mix a little black with the yellow to create a spooky green tinge.

2 Starting above the inner corner of the eye, paint a sharp diagonal line in black, sweeping up toward the temples. Carefully feather the top edge of the line, using small sharp strokes to suggest a coarse hairy eyebrow.

3 Paint the eyelids and inner corners of the eyes in dark brown, extending the color down the sides of the nose to a point just above each nostril.

4 Start to create the folds and creases in the face; take the dark brown paint down along the folds of the cheeks to a point level with the mouth. Paint bags under the eyes by following the lower line of the eye socket at both the inner and outer corners. Feather all these lines with a damp brush.

— HALLOWEEN —

Tip: When trying to age a young face, only apply lines in a downward direction – lines that are drawn upward will only lift the face and counteract the effect you are hoping for.

5 Add some creases across the forehead and two vertical frown lines. Blend these lines slightly with a cotton swab.

6 Paint some small wrinkles around the outer corners of the eyes and shade the hollows of the cheeks to make them look sunken.

— HALLOWEEN —

7 Small black semicircles on both top and bottom lids will give a beady-eyed look.

8 Block the mouth in brown and draw a crooked black line across the lips, dropping the ends down at each corner of the mouth.

9 Add some fine wrinkle lines all round the mouth and a touch of shading to the cleft of the chin.

10 The wicked witch is finished, and the model will hardly recognize herself – so watch out!

— CARNIVAL —

Batman

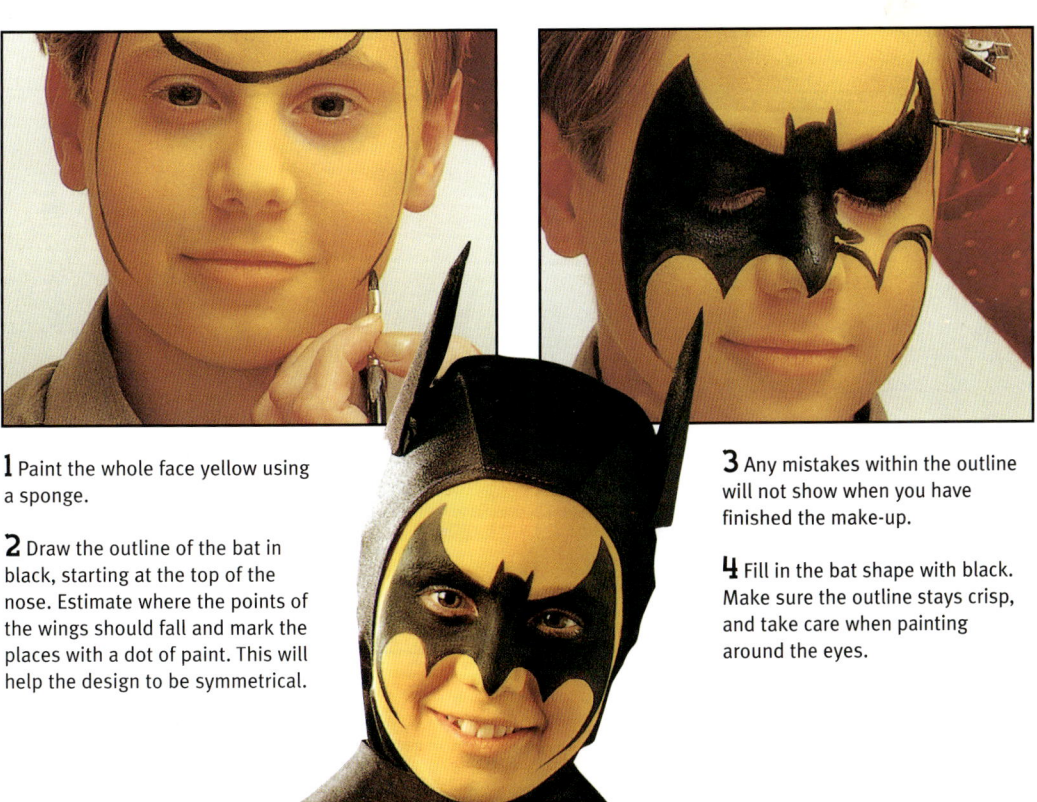

1 Paint the whole face yellow using a sponge.

2 Draw the outline of the bat in black, starting at the top of the nose. Estimate where the points of the wings should fall and mark the places with a dot of paint. This will help the design to be symmetrical.

3 Any mistakes within the outline will not show when you have finished the make-up.

4 Fill in the bat shape with black. Make sure the outline stays crisp, and take care when painting around the eyes.

— CARNIVAL —

Cowboy

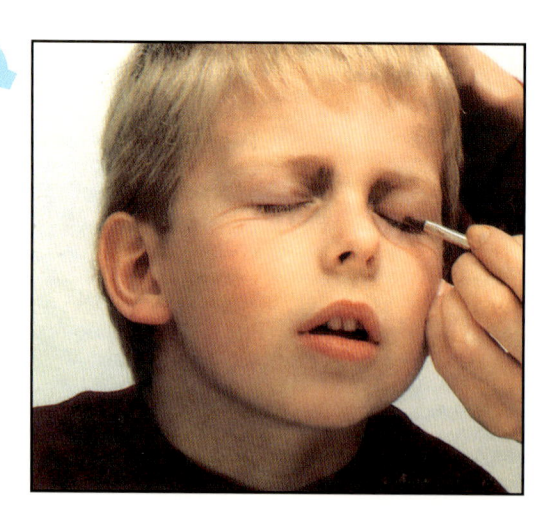

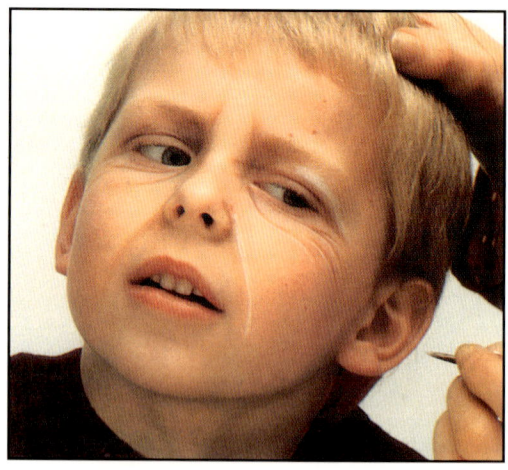

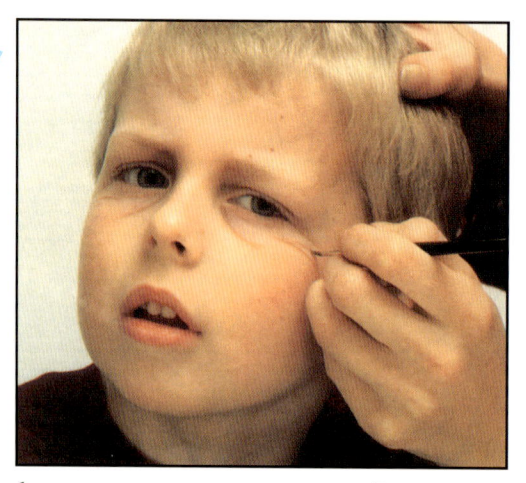

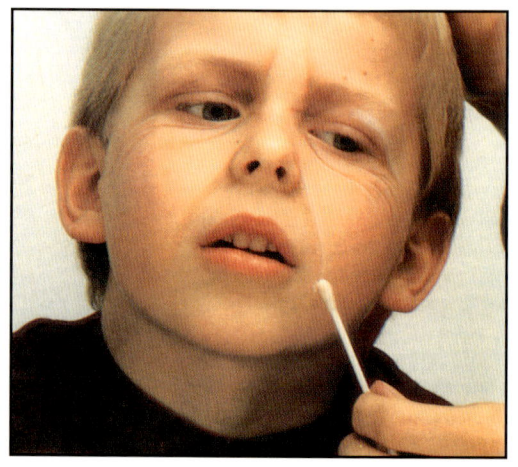

1 Using a thin brush and brown paint, shade the eyelid and the inner corner of the eye, blending the color down the sides of the nose slightly. Add a subtle line of color to the lower part of the eye socket.

2 Add some wrinkle lines in their natural positions: downward from the outer corner of the eye, from the nose down to the corners of the mouth, in the crease of the chin, and across the forehead, as well as two vertical frown lines above the eyebrows.

3 Highlight the lines and wrinkles by painting a little white alongside them. To make the eyelids look droopy, paint a white diagonal line along the fold of the upper lid, starting at the eyebrow and ending below the outer corner of the eye.

4 Softly blend any hard edges using the corner of a slightly dampened sponge.

— CARNIVAL —

5 Create an unshaven look by stippling the beard and mustache area with a coarse sponge and some brown paint (see instructions on page 9). Build up the effect gradually, using only a small amount of color. Dab the sponge on the back of your hand to remove any excess paint. Darken the eyebrows if necessary. This subtle make-up will enhance any cowboy dress-up costume.

— CARNIVAL —

Pirate

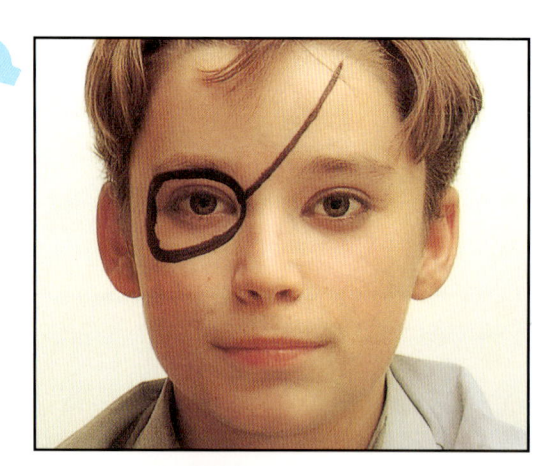

1 Draw the outline of the eye patch with a fine brush.

2 Fill in the outline with black and draw in the ties.

3 Create an unshaven look by stippling black paint gently onto the lower face with a sponge (see instructions on page 9).

Tip: Build up the color gradually and don't overdo it.

— CARNIVAL —

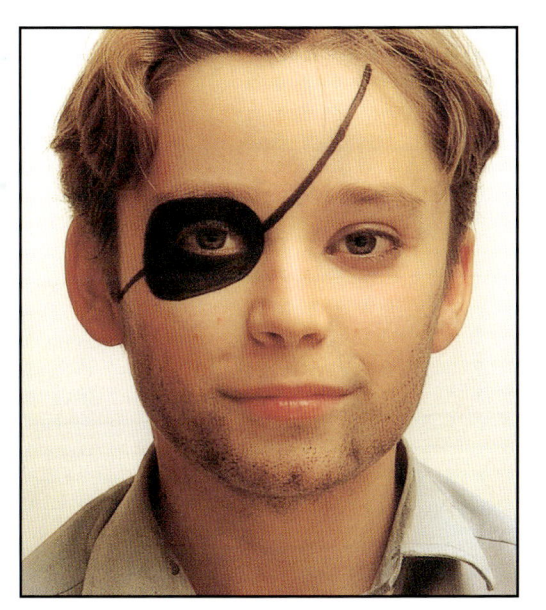

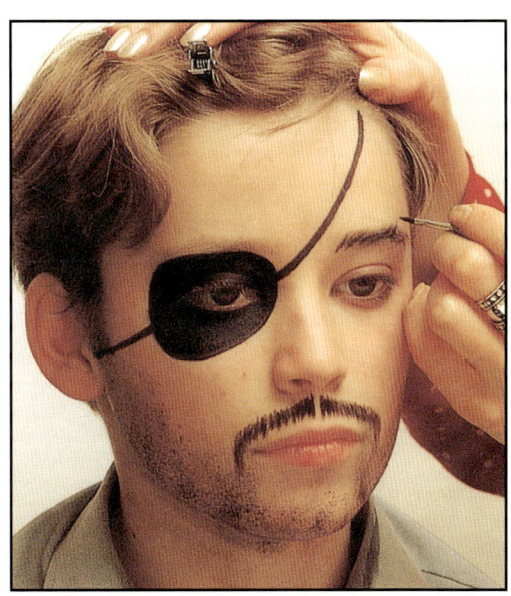

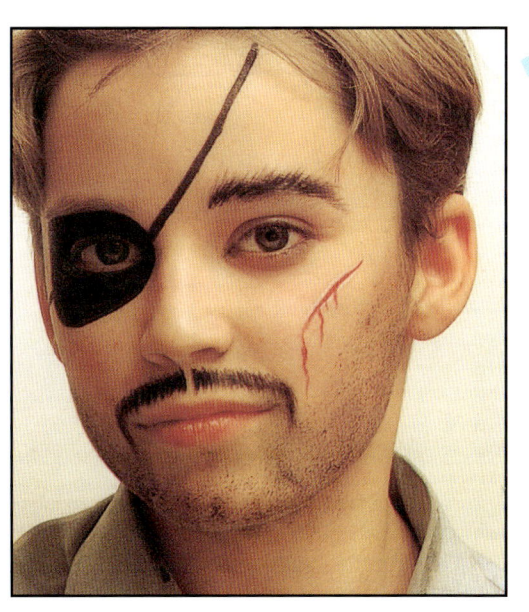

4 A realistic five o'clock shadow is beginning to emerge.

5 Carefully paint on the mustache with a very fine brush using small sharp strokes.

6 Emphasize the model's eyebrows using the same sharp brush technique as before.

7 Create a scar by painting a thin dark red line and outlining it in white to achieve a 3-D effect. Paint on a few drops of fake blood.

— CARNIVAL —

Spiderman

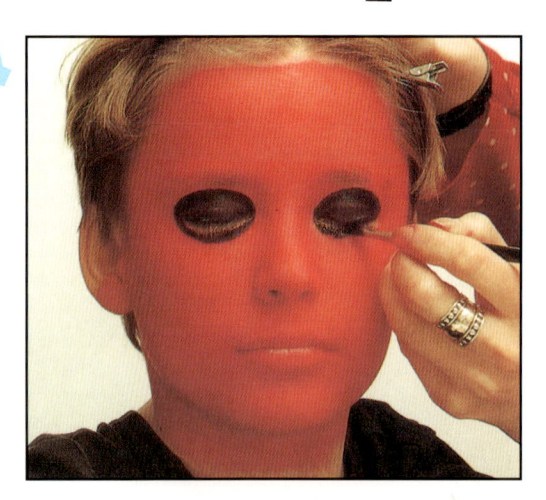

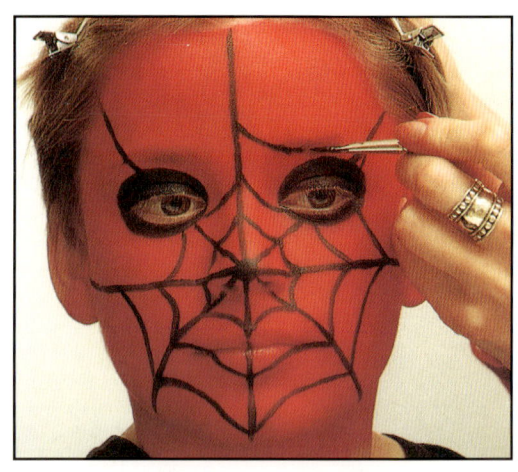

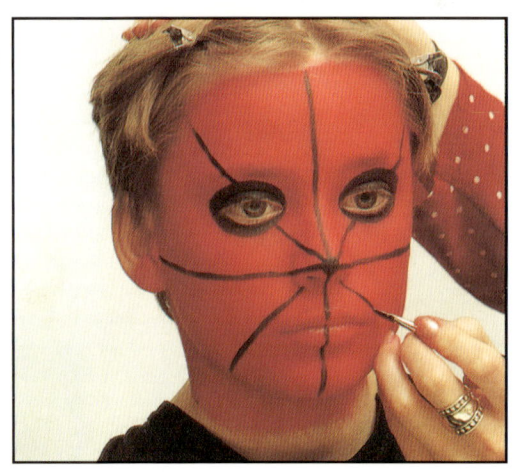

1 Cover the face and neck with red paint using a sponge. Fill in the eye socket area above and below the eye in black.

2 Make a dot on the end of the nose and use it as a center point to draw four thin black lines across the face as follows:
1 right down the center of the face; 2 straight across the face from ear to ear; 3 left to right diagonally from forehead to chin; and 4 right to left diagonally.

3 Begin to develop the web, starting near the center and repeating the pattern at regular intervals.

4 The web continues right to the edge of the face.